Goodbye Writer's Block

How to Be a Creative Genius and Have an Abundance of Ideas Plus the Inspiration and Motivation to Write

New and Improved Edition

By Ruth Barringham

Published by Cheriton House Publishing

Australia

Copyright © 2014 Ruth Barringham

All rights reserved.

This edition updated 2023

This publication is copyrighted and must not be loaned out, sold or otherwise distributed by anyone other than the publisher.

This work is copyright. Apart from any use under the Copyright Act 1968, no part may be reproduced by any process, nor may any other exclusive right be exercised without the permission of Ruth Barringham.

This book is sold subject to the condition that it shall not, by way of trade or otherwise, be lent, re-sold, hired out or otherwise circulated without the author's prior consent in any form of binding or cover other than that with which it is published and without a similar condition including this condition being imposed on the subsequent purchaser.

ISBN: Paperback: 978-0-6457543-0-8
eBook: 978-0-6457543-1-5

Also by Ruth Barringham

How to Quit Smoking

How To Write an Article In 15 Minutes Or Less

7 Day eBook Writing and Publishing System

Living The Laptop Lifestyle

Mission Critical for Life

Self Publish Worldwide

The 12 Month Writing Challenge

How To Have More Money Now

Stop Procrastinating

The Monthly Challenge Writing Series

Book 1 - Quick Cash Freelance Writing

Book 2 - Build A Lucrative Niche Website

Book 3 - Fast & Profitable Article Writing

Book 4 - The One Month Author

See more of my books at
https://www.cheritonhousepublishing.com

Disclaimer:

The Author and Publisher have used their best efforts in preparing this book. The Author and Publisher make no representation or warranties with respect to the accuracy, applicability, fitness, or completeness of the contents of this book.

The information contained in this book is strictly for information purposes. Therefore, if you wish to apply ideas contained in this book, you are taking full responsibility for your actions. Whilst we hope you find the contents of this book interesting and informative; the contents are for general information purposes only and do not constitute advice. We believe the contents to be true and accurate as at the date of writing but can give no assurances or warranty regarding the accuracy, currency, or applicability of any of the contents in relation to specific situations and particular circumstances.

Any links to third party websites are provided solely for the purpose of your convenience. Links made to websites are made at your own risk and the Author and Publisher accept no liability for any linked sites. When you access a website, please understand that it is independent from the Author and Publisher and the Author and Publisher have no control over the content of that website.

Further, a link contained in this book does not mean that the Author or Publisher endorses or accepts any responsibility for the content or the use of such website. The Author and Publisher do not give any representation regarding the quality, safety, suitability, or reliability of any of them or any of the material contained within them. Users must take their own precautions to ensure that what is selected for use is free of such items as viruses, worms, trojan horses and other items of a destructive nature.

All websites, products and services are mentioned, without warranty of any kind, either express or implied, including, but not limited to, the implied warranties of merchant ability and fitness for a particular purpose.

Table of Contents

Why Do Writers Write?..1
How to Find a Plethora of Ideas 4
Finding Ideas for Non-Fiction Writing 7
Finding Ideas for Fiction Writing 14
Reversing Ideas..22
How to Get More Ideas...24
Suffering From Idea Overload 25
How To Do It All...28
So What Happens Now? 32

Why Do Writers Write?

Why do you write?

Have you ever asked yourself this question?

The answer is always the same. You write because you want to/have to write. It's just like any creative person, whether they're artists, musicians, sculptors, knitters, dressmakers, or even cake decorators, they do what they do because they can't NOT do it.

A writer deprived of a writing implement, is a sad person indeed. Many writers carry a notebook with them wherever they go, just like a smoker will carry cigarettes, because when the urge takes them, or they find themselves with some free time, they just have to write.

Does this sound like you? Do you love to write and when you sit down and start working hours can fly by while you're deeply entrenched in your work?

Does the thought of not being able to write fill you with dread?

If you're a writer, you write. You don't need a reason.

But here's another question. If you always want to write, then why does it sometimes seem so difficult?

Why is it that you know you want to write, but you don't have the motivation and focus to actually sit down and write every day?

If these are any of the problems that you're suffering from then read on.

What is Writer's Block?

It happens to all writers at some point, and sometimes it happens often.

You want to write. You need to sit down and write because you have a lot of work to do and deadlines are looming.

Or maybe you're a blogger and you need to write more content for your blog, but you've written about the same subject for so long that you feel like you've run out of things to say about it.

So you knuckle-drag your way over to your writing desk, sit down, open your computer, or take out your notebook and pen... and then nothing. You don't know what to do next.

So you take out your work from the previous day and read through it but still you can't think of what to do next.

Has this ever happened to you?

Has it ever happened to you more than once?

Then I have the solution for you right here within these pages.

So keep reading.

But don't just read. Take action.

If you follow all the advice in this book you'll never be lost for ideas again and you'll be able to sit down and write anytime, even when you really don't feel like it and the ideas just won't come.

And anytime you do feel the desire to write, you'll be able to sit down and start writing straight away and have the motivation and focus to write for hours. Really!

Can you imagine how this will change your life completely?

Just think of how great it's going to be when you can sit and write every day with an abundance of ideas, maximum focus, and you're always brimming with motivation and inspiration.

Not only that, but because you'll be writing more than you ever have before, your writing income will increase too. You'll eventually be able to quit your job and write full time, knowing that you'll be able to write every day, no matter what.

On the other hand, if you read through this book, close it, and do nothing, then nothing will change, and you'll stay stuck in the same position you are now, week after week, month after month, and year after year.

You'll keep wishing you had an unlimited supply of ideas, you'll want to sit down and write very day, yet you'll do nothing except go to bed every evening wondering why you even bothered.

Remember the old saying:

"Regret weighs tons."

But if you were writing consistently, you could even have time to start a blog about your writing and use it as a place to advertise your books too.

At the moment though, you're not doing the writing you should be doing and you're probably reading the blogs of other writers which makes you feel as though other writers are always writing more than you and that you'll never catch up.

Yet you just know that if the ideas would keep flowing, you'd be able to write a whole library of books and sell them worldwide.

But you don't have any ideas, so... there's always the day job that you've had for years that you can keep for many more.

But you don't want this do you? You want to be a writer, but the lack of ideas is holding you back.

So this is it.

This is where you throw off the shackles of so-called "Writer's Block" and find your creative writing genius so that you'll have a lifetime's worth of ideas for writing plus the inspiration and motivation to write every day.

Are you ready?

Then let's get going.

How to Find a Plethora of Ideas

If you want to write, then you need to start writing. It's as simple as that.

It's also as difficult as that too because how can you sit down and write if you don't have any idea of what to write about?

Well wonder no more.

Whether you want to write fiction or non-fiction, I'm going to show you how to find ideas of what to write about. And it won't cost you anything except a small amount of your time.

First Things First

First of all you need to generate the necessary self-discipline to take the first step

And that means you have to actually sit down and write. Your writing needs to be a habit, preferably a daily habit.

It's no good telling yourself that you'll fit your writing in when you have the time. That time will never come.

We often tell ourselves that we're going to do something "later," or "soon," or "someday." But the words later, soon and someday are simply another way of saying never.

Next time you tell yourself you'll sit down and write later/soon/someday, remember that what you're really saying is "I'm never going to start writing." You're just fooling yourself if you think otherwise.

So the question is, what are you going to do about it?

What you need is a plan. Once you have a plan you can follow it.

Start with a goal and make sure you also have a deadline. And it needs to be reasonable for you to do.

For instance, maybe you'll say, "I want to write and publish a book every 3 months."

That's a good goal because it's achievable and it has a deadline. But you'll also need to factor in other things too, like book cover design, formatting, publishing, and marketing. Not to mention all the other writing projects you usually do. Or you probably have a day job you have to go to every day, so you're writing time will be limited to only a few hours a day in the evenings, or you may get up early to write every day.

I know of many writers who get up at 4 am every day and write for 2 or 3 hours. They say it starts their day in the right way, plus it's the quietest time of the day with less distractions, especially if the rest of the family are still in bed. They know that whatever else comes up during the day, the most important task, their writing, is already done.

Other writers work in the evenings because they love to settle down to writing once the dishes are done and the kids are in bed. They prefer writing to drinking and binge-watching Netflix.

But you'll already know if you're a morning person or a burning the midnight oil type of person. Some writers use their lunch hour at work to get their writing done.

Knowing if you're a morning or evening person will help you to decide how you're going to achieve your goal. So you might say,

"Every day I'm going to sit down and write for an hour before I go to work."

Or

"Every day I'm going to sit down and write 2,000 words after dinner."

Once you have your plan then all you have to do is follow it and you'll reach your goal without too much effort. You just need to be consistent.

Commit to working your plan for at least one month just to see how it goes. Or if one month seems like too much, commit to trying it for one full week. That should be enough time for you to show yourself just how productive you can be.

So once you have your plan and your commitment to stick to it for a while to see how it goes, you're ready to start writing.

Except...

You still don't know what to write about. You need ideas.

And now I'll tell you how to find them.

Finding Ideas for Non-Fiction Writing

If you want to write non-fiction, then you need to decide what niche you will be writing in. Or if all you want to do is write books, you can, if you want to, write in several different niche.

There is one writer who writes Kindle eBooks and he's written over 190 so far (at time of writing but the numbers are still increasing). His books are in many different niches, including (but in no way limited to) future concepts, national defense, economics, business, self-help, humanitarian causes and community nonprofit groups, writing, and publishing. He also writes science fiction novels. He describes himself as an overachiever and he's not wrong.

His name is Lance Winslow (you can look him up on Amazon to see just how many books he's written). Not only is he a prolific author, he's also a retired franchisee (he owned 187 franchises), runs a think tank, and has written over 31,000 online articles that collectively add up to over 10 million words.

This is a guy who just writes what he wants to write and doesn't listen to anyone else about what he should write or how to write it. Many writing "experts" will tell you that to be successful you need to write in just one niche or one genre and stick to it. But Lance Winslow clearly doesn't listen to that advice and just writes on subjects he's passionate about.

And as you can imagine, he writes a lot. He is one of the most prolific, yet unknown, writers I've ever come across. If you want to write like he does, take a look at just one of his eBooks, **"Speed Reading and Rapid Writing."** You can find it at https://amzn.to/3SmUJCv.

Most writers prefer to be known as an expert on just one subject. But writing in 700 different niches is working for Lance Winslow so anything is possible.

But whatever your chosen niche, you still need to find ideas to write about.

And these are some places to start looking:

Forums.

These are great places to find ideas to write about. Just do a Google search of your chosen niche plus the word forum. For instance, when I was researching for this book, I did a Google search for "writing forum."

Forums are great for researching just about any topic. But as a word of warning, if you can't find a forum for your chosen topic, chances are that if no one is talking about it online, it's because no one is interested.

Once you find a few forums you can look at which topics are the most popular. You can tell which are popular, because they have the most threads started, and the longest discussions.

For this book, I searched a few writing forums and noticed a lot of discussion on writer's block so that's what I decided to make this book about.

But before I started searching, I only knew that I was going to write a book about writing. I chose writing because it's something I know a lot about and it's a subject I love to write about.

My research on the forums narrowed down my search about writing to the smaller niche of writer's block. And you can do the same.

Start with a general topic and narrow it down to a tighter sub-topic. For instance, if you wanted to write on the subject of 'how to be a manager', narrowing it down to a tighter sub-topic of 'how to be a hotel manager' might be an easier subject to write about.

Likewise, if, say you wanted to write about dogs, by searching "dog forum" you could narrow your topic down to dog training, breeds, behaviour, etc.

Just a quick Google search right now produced a dog forum (called exactly that, dogforum.com) where there are also threads for dog grooming, health, food, gear, shows, working dogs, performance, sports, art, stories, memorials and pictures.

This is just one example of how useful forums can be for research and sparking ideas.

You can literally spend hours searching through forums and taking notes because it's amazing how much information you can find once you start looking. You can even find enough information for a whole series of books.

Forums are also great for showing you the jargon that people in that niche are using.

To begin, just think of something that you enjoy or are enthusiastic about, such as hiking, war planes, parenting, cooking, baking, car restoration, doll collecting, drawing, black and white movies, fashion, rug making... It really doesn't matter what it is. It just needs to be something you are interested in, or passionate about, or maybe something you'd like to learn about.

I recently looked up knitting forums and came across dozens of sites. There was even a forum about 3D knitting. I had no idea that even existed. But just a simple subject as knitting threw up plenty of ideas like history of knitting, random point knitting (never heard of that either), knitting patterns, machine knitting, knitting classes, and there is even a forum about knitting on planes.

But it just goes to show how many sub-niches you can find once you start looking.

Magazine Headlines.

One thing about magazine editors is that they know how to write intriguing headlines, in particular the ones that you see on the magazine covers.

The best magazine headlines for researching are usually found of Reader's Digest magazine. As a quick example, the current headlines on the cover are, Why does money cause anxiety? 10 surprising conditions your hands might predict, Neurology professors just listed the 9 worst habits for the human brain, Is only child syndrome real? I've worked on cruise ships for 10 years – these are the mistakes every traveler should avoid.

Those are quite diverse topics and may or may not be suitable for giving you an idea of something to write about, but if you search magazines in your own niche, you'll probably find something.

You can also look at the magazine's Table of Contents as well. There are many more articles inside the magazine than what is listed on the cover.

You can also delve right into the magazine content too because sometimes even something as simple as a letter to the editor can spark an idea for a book.

Amazon Book Search.

Amazon is a great website for research. You can browse all the books (both digital and print) to see what is available, what's selling the most, and what is not popular.

Amazon search bar can help, because as you type in your search keywords, it prompts you with popular search words much the same as Google does.

This is helpful because you can see what others are searching for as well as what's available. And remember that people searching Amazon are buyers, so they're not just idly browsing like people doing a Google search. This means that what they're looking for is also what they want to buy.

You can also use the 'look inside' feature to scan the Table of Contents of similar books to the one you're thinking of writing. Even if you don't have a book in mind, just looking around at what others are writing can help to give you plenty of ideas for your own writing.

Another feature on Amazon that is useful for research is their "customers who bought this item also bought..." which gives you even more books you can search through. Amazon is really helpful when it comes to online search and prompts you and makes suggestions all the time. So use them.

Once you start searching, even if you don't know what you're looking for, ideas will start to generate and inspiration will start to strike. You just have to start looking.

Blogs.

These are a great place for inspiration and ideas. Sometimes I'll read an article on someone's blog and think that they've only just touched the surface of the amount of information to be written on that particular subject. This will prompt me with an idea for a new book.

Some blogs have long articles on them that can be extremely informational. If you find a blog like this, it's possible to gather a few articles from there for brainstorming your own book.

And by 'gather' I mean collect them into a folder on your computer or copy and paste them into a document. I actually have a folder on my computer called 'Book Ideas' and it's full of notes taken from blogs and other websites as well as my own ideas of what to do with the information I've gathered as well as all my thoughts about it. Idea gathering really is addictive once you start.

The best types of articles are the list type such as "10 Things You Need to know" or "12 Simple Steps". These can be particularly helpful because if it's a really interesting article you can expand each topic in the list into a whole chapter in a book or mix and match topics from different lists.

Or you could think of a better list of your own. Some bloggers publish eBooks that are nothing more than a group of articles from their blog, formatted into chapters and published.

And there's no reason you can't do the same if you find enough articles on different topics of the same subject and it provides you with enough ideas for your own book.

Just remember that while you're gathering ideas and information, perform your own 'due diligence' if it's a topic that you're not familiar with, just to make sure that the information is accurate.

Also remember that I'm not telling you to plagiarize someone else's work. You're just using what you find online for research and to provide you with your own ideas. So don't copy what you find. Write your own stuff in your own way.

Be authentic and be original in everything you write. While you might be using the ideas from someone else's articles, you're writing your own stuff. Their ideas must only be used to spark bigger and better ideas of your own.

And if you search online for ideas using forums, magazines, Amazon and blogs and you still can't come up with anything - nada, nothing, zip, zilch, - then you're really not trying because real writers are always finding fresh ideas everywhere. While others make excuse after excuse as to why they're not writing.

Random Article Ideas Generator

This is a quick way to find an idea for a blog post if you don't have one.

Do a quick online search for "article ideas generator" or "blog ideas generator" or something similar.

If you're writing non-fiction, you usually know what subject or niche you need to write about. You use a random generator to come up with headline ideas within that subject or niche.

Of course, most of the ideas they come up with won't be suitable, but it can spark other ideas.

I went onto a random content generator just now and submitted ideas for the phrase "earn money writing." It came back with "10 Tips to Help You Earn More Writing Income." Not bad and it took me less than a minute to go online find that.

Numbers in a headline, as in "10 Tips..." always attract attention because people are always looking for ways to do something and if you can offer multiple ways, you'll get their attention.

You can also use numbers to come up with chapters of a book, or a list of points to bring up in a lengthy article.

It works like this. You know what you have to write about, so list 10 questions people might ask you about the topic.

So if you were asked to write about business meetings, some of the questions you might be asked would be:

Why do people have business meetings?

How long do meetings last?

How can you keep meetings short?

How do meetings benefit the business?

What would happen if there were no meetings?

Which employees attend meetings?

Do all businesses have meetings?

Where are business meetings conducted?

As you can tell from that list, I know nothing about business meetings because I always worked in retail and commercial cleaning before I became a writer so business meetings didn't really happen.

But not knowing about business meetings probably works in my favour because I know what questions to ask because I've never been to one. But no matter what the subject, there are always questions that can be asked about it. And these days finding answers is easy.

Finding Ideas for Fiction Writing

Finding ideas for your next great novel is easy because ideas can be all around you. All you need is a prompt which can be anything within your range of vision.

For instance, as I sit here and type I can see the Himalayan Salt Lamp on the desk glowing its calming orange colour, so I could use that as a story prompt. If I wanted to write a horror story it could be about a salt lamp that always glows at night when something scary is about to happen. Or it could be a romance novel where the salt lamp is a poignant reminder of a lost love. Or a thriller where the murder victim is always left lying in the orange glow of a salt lamp and the police later discover that the lamps are a clue to the killer's identity. Or there is a maniac who hits his victims in the mouth with a salt lamp and breaks their teeth (phew! Boy do I have an active imagination, and these lamps are supposed to make me feel relaxed).

But you get the idea. Writing prompts are all around you.

There Are No New Plots

If you're worried that you don't have an original plot, don't worry. There are no new plots. But what you have going for you, is your unique way of telling a story.

Let's just look at a few instances of same plot - new story.

There was a TV show years ago called The Honeymooners. When you animate that show and you have the Flintstones.

I used to watch an old TV show called, My Favorite Martian, about a man who had to hide his Martian friend by pretending it was his uncle.

Years later the Martian character became a comedian in the new show Mork and Mindy about a woman who hides her Martian friend, Mork, by pretending he's her human friend.

Then Mork became aa puppet in a new show about an alien called Alf. Later still, another TV show about 3 aliens living together, was called Third rock From the Sun.

And look at the movie "Independence Day" with Will Smith. It's nothing more than a story based on the older movie, "War of the Worlds" which is a based on the H G Wells book of the same name.

In War of the Worlds, Martians invade the world. In the newer movie, we call them aliens.

In War of the Worlds, the Martians die from a human bacterium virus.

In "Independence Day," the aliens die because they cannot defend against a computer virus.

And just look at the similarities between the original Star Wars movie and Harry Potter and the Philosopher's Stone.

Luke Skywalker (Harry Potter) is an orphan living with his aunt and uncle in the wilderness (suburbia).

Luke (Harry) is rescued from aliens (muggles) by a wise and bearded Ben Kenobi (Hagrid) who turns out to be a Jedi Knight (wizard).

Ben (Hagrid) tells Luke (Harry) that his father was also a Jedi Knight (wizard) and was also one of the best ever pilots (Quidditch players).

Luke (Harry) is taught how to use a light saber (magic wand) and he trains to become a Jedi (wizard) just like his father.

Luke (Harry) has many adventures in space (Hogwarts) and meets two good friends, Han Solo (Ron Weasley) and Princess Leia (Hermione).

Luke (Harry) also becomes the best pilot (Quidditch player) in the Battle of the Death Star (Quidditch match).

Luke (Harry) has to ultimately fight with Darth Vader (Lord Voldemort) who, it turns out, killed his aunt and uncle (parents).

I hope you can see from just these few examples how one plot can be made into many different stories.

So now let's look at some of the places where you can find thousands of plots.

The Library.

You can go to your local library and have a search through the fiction section. You don't need to read every book. Find a story idea that appeals to you just by looking at the title, the cover image, or the blurb on the back cover. Just doing this can help to give you plenty of ideas for fleshing it out into a complete novel of your own.

Or try this. Pick a novel at random. Look at the picture on the cover. Come up with a story based on the picture. Your story idea doesn't even have to be in the same genre as the book. You might see a picture of a romantic couple, but instead of embracing, he's stabbing her, or she's dying and whispering a secret in his ear, or it's a mugging, or he's desperately trying to talk her out of doing something dangerous, or she's evil and she won't let go of him, or she's looking into his eyes and stealing his soul.

Whatever it is, look at the cover image, and come up with a completely different idea than what the picture is supposed to be conveying.

Secondhand Books.

A browse at the books in a thrift shop can also help you find ideas for a story of your own. And even if you wanted to take one home to read, it would probably only cost you 50 cents to buy.

In these types of stores you can find really old books that have a really promising story idea but because of the age of the book, it wasn't as well written as it could have been. By that I mean that there were more restrictions on content and description back 'in those days' which means that you could take an old story and breathe new life into it.

Make sure you look for a book by a relatively unknown author. Read the story and see what you didn't like about it and figure out how it could have been better and then set out mapping out your own novel. Most of the old books by unknown authors that end up in thrift stores are often there because they're not great stories, but there is room for improvement to make it a blockbuster best seller.

Again, keep in mind that I'm not tell you to plagiarize someone else's work. But you can use the essence of the story to come up with a better one of your own.

Amazon Search and Free eBooks.

Gotta love Amazon for letting us browse books so easily. When you're on their website you can read book titles, look at the cover, read the blurb, read a few pages, and even download free eBooks.

This is a great way to get ideas for your own novels. For instance, say you download a free eBook because you think the story sounds promising and you like the title. But when you read it, it isn't what you thought it was going to be. So you write the novel that you were hoping for instead. See? Instant idea generator.

Or you might like the story premise but think the ending was weak or the book wasn't long enough and didn't have enough detail. So you write it your own way with more detail and a great ending. You might even have enough ideas to write a whole series of novels.

That's the great thing about having a creative mind is that it can take just one little thing to spark a whole plethora of ideas. But you have to start searching as many places as you can, especially other novels.

This is why writers are always readers as well. We read something and think "I could have written that better." And then we do it.

Re-writing An Old Story.

There are plenty of ideas to be gotten from old stories that can be rewritten or made modern.

I recently went to see a musical called "Jesus Christ Superstar." I'd seen the same show many years ago at the cinema and as you can guess, it's the story of the life of Jesus, with lots of singing, hence it's a musical.

But this new show was different to the old story because it was set in modern times and Jesus was living in the city and preaching to people in the ghettos.

And you could do something similar. I don't mean copy what's already been done, but update it, bring an old story back to life but in modern times and with a different (or similar) ending.

Say you wrote a story about the life of Jesus but it was set in modern times. His name wasn't Jesus, it was Ralph and he lived in a normal suburban home and wore a robe, and everyone thought he was nuts because he claimed to be the son of God.

But maybe there were little tell-tale occurrences that made people think that maybe he wasn't so crazy after all. Maybe he preached to people in bars and turned their drinks into wine but everyone thought he was just a magician. Can you see how this story could be developed?

You could use other well-known stories and change them too, such as a murder that takes place on a moving train, or a creepy modern-day Rumpelstiltskin, or a reworking of the story of The Monkey's Paw.

No doubt you get the idea by now.

Ideas for fiction stories can be found everywhere.

Writing Prompts

These are great to use if you're ever stuck for a story idea. A prompt can be a few words or an image.

I remember when I was at school, both elementary school and high school. The teacher would show us a picture and tell us to write a story about it. Or they'd tell us to write a story that had a lot of action in it, or a story with a scary moment in it. They would also use situational prompts like a haunted house, or a boat, or a forest.

Personally, I found writing prompts extremely useful and once I had an idea, which didn't take long, I start writing and keep going for the rest of the lesson and finish my story at home if I didn't have enough time to finish it at school.

And I still find writing prompts useful. My favourite type are freelance submission guidelines. I enjoy submitting freelance work and I use the guidelines for what the publication is looking for as a prompt for what to write, the same way I used to do it at school.

To find some of your own, just do an online search for "writing prompts." It will throw up hundreds of results. But don't just look for a prompt. Start working on it straight away while the ideas are fresh in your mind. If it prompts a book idea, flesh out an outline. If it's a short story idea, write it straight away, or outline it and get back to it as soon as you can.

The Guaranteed Way to Start Writing

This is a fun thing to do and no matter how much you feel you're not in the mood to write, or you think you can never think of an idea to write, this will get you writing immediately.

I call it The 5-Minute Writing Exercise.

Do this, and you can't NOT write. Not only that, but in the 5 minutes that you're going to be writing, you should be able to write 2/3 of a page of writing.

Don't just read this part, do the work. I guarantee you'll be amazed at how creative your mind can be once you're under the pump to write, and you'll also be amazed at how much you're capable of writing in just 5 minutes. Once you try this 5-minute writing exercise, you'll want to do it again and again.

Here's what you need to do:

- Go online and do a search for a random word generator.
- Obtain 3 random words.
- Set a timer for 5 minutes.
- Write for 5 minutes until your timer sounds.

- You must use your 3 random words in the first paragraph. You can use them more than once but all 3 must be in your opening paragraph.
- When the timer sounds stop writing, even if you're part way through a sentence.
- You should have written 2/3 of an A4 page.

And that's it. That's all it takes to get you writing immediately no matter if you feel like writing or not and even if you don't have any idea what to write about.

Sometimes when I do this exercise I have no idea how I'm going to use the 3 random words because they at first they seem so unconnected. But it only takes me a few seconds to come up with an idea.

The reason it's quick for me to think of a story idea using the 3 random words is the time crunch. I only have seconds to think about it as I set my timer and then I only have 5 minutes to write. So I write without a clue where I'm going with it, and yet somehow the ideas evolve as I write.

I recently did this exercise and the 3 random words I was given were 'scorch, magenta, library.' I thought these were terrible words and I was tempted to spin again to get 3 different words. But I stuck with it and wrote for 5 minutes.

My opening paragraph containing the 3 words was as follows:

"Rebecca always thought that if the sky glowed red at dusk, the following day would be hot enough to scorch the earth. Tonight, as she hurried to the local library before it closed, the sky was an eerie magenta."

I thought it wasn't bad. I then went on writing about her going into the library, why she'd gone there and what she did. My mind was a blur as the ideas just kept coming.

I ended up being pretty pleased with my 2/3 page of writing and the next night I picked up the notebook I'd written it in and over the next few nights, I carried on the story and ended up writing a 5,000-word short story.

I've filed it on my computer ready for a submission opportunity which I'm sure will turn up one day. My computer has quite a few unpublished works stored on it as well as many published works.

And it's all because I keep on finding ideas and I'm always working on my next writing project.

And when I've got nothing to write, I do another 5-minute writing exercise, and as before, the ideas start flowing.

Reversing Ideas

This is a great way to generate ideas for your writing and it works for both fiction and non-fiction.

The way to do it is to think of the ending, or the big climax of the story, and reverse engineer it to work out how it happened or how it can be done.

For fiction it's easy. Just think of an ending to a story, even if it's just the last line. And then think of how on earth that could have transpired and work backwards to figure it out.

Or if you have an idea for the main crisis of a story, work backwards to figure out who all the characters will be in the story and how they came to the crux of the story and what all the subplots are and how it will all overlap.

So if you're writing a murder mystery, you might start with the scene of the murder and work out who all the suspects are, what they all have to do with the victim's life and who is the eventual killer and why. It's like connecting the dots.

You don't need to know every detail to begin plotting out a novel. You just start with one idea or one ending and reverse engineer it all to figure it all out, probably using a lot of "what if?" questions.

You can use reversing ideas for non-fiction too. You just think of an idea of how to do something, without actually knowing if it can be done. For instance, say you want to write a book about how to write an eBook every week, publish and promote it, make sales, and still have time for a life.

You then figure out how it can be done and the timings of everything, try it out yourself, and then write up how to do it.

Your idea has to be something that at first sounds impossible to do, but it's something that everyone would like to be able to do. Then you figure out how it can be done. It could be a cook book about how to make 100 different meals with just 6 basic ingredients. Or how to clean your whole house in 2 hours without breaking into a sweat. Or the no-maintenance garden. Or how to lose 2 kilos in a week. But be careful of that last one. It could be a health and safety issue.

Just think of something that you'd like to do, or that others would be interested in, and then research and test how it can be done.

This is the same way that magicians work. They think of a trick that seems impossible to do, and then they reverse engineer a way to do it.

How to Get More Ideas

Sometimes, the only way to get more ideas is to slow down your manic, crazy mind. If you're rushed, stressed and overwhelmed with worry, frantic to find the next great idea, it's hard to be creative.

Sometimes you need to walk away from your computer and take a complete break from writing and go do something physical instead. It's often during these times that writers have "Eureka" moments.

These breaks from writing are great for catching up with other jobs around the home like washing the car, mowing the lawn or cleaning the windows.

You can also try listening to relaxing music while you write and research, although horror writer, Stephen King, listens to heavy metal music while he writes. For me though, there's nothing like meditation music or brain entrainment audios for helping me to concentrate.

It works two ways by helping me to stay focused on my work and by blocking out other noises that might distract me. They have really helped me to write more over the last few years by keeping me focused and keeping my creative spark burning.

I just plug my ear buds into my ears, select one of my relaxation audios, start writing and get totally engrossed in my work, forgetting about everything else as I write.

Suffering From Idea Overload

This is the opposite of writer's block. Instead of having no ideas, you have a mind bursting with so many ideas that you don't know which one to use first and so you end up using none.

I have this problem quite often. It usually happens when I'm doing the cleaning or the ironing or out walking. All of a sudden a great idea will pop into my head. Then I'll think on it more until it's such a brilliant idea that I can't wait to start it.

The only problem though, is that I'm already working on other writing projects but now I want to start this new one.

So I write down my idea and get so enthusiastic that I want to start it straight away. But instead I have to sit down and work on my current projects. But the new idea won't leave me and I keep thinking about it and can't concentrate on my current projects.

Then I'll get another idea and then I'll want to work on that one too. But I'm still working on other projects. So I finish what I'm working on but it's too late. I didn't flesh out my first idea enough on paper and I didn't write down my second idea at all so that one is gone.

Over the years I've learnt that the best thing to do with idea overload is to write down your idea straight away. If you're out somewhere and you can't write it down, like when you're out walking or driving, then use your audio recorder on your phone to record your idea.

The best thing to do is always have a note book handy to write down all your ideas and a short summary of what you want to write. Some of my notes on my ideas get a bit long but making too many notes is better than not writing enough. If you're out, write down your idea as soon as you get back. Or if you're driving, write down your idea as soon as you park. Keep a notebook and a few pens in your glove box ready for any ideas you get, or for writing whenever you get the urge.

I have one notebook that I use expressly for ideas. I'm on my second notebook now and I haven't used all the ideas in my first one yet. Sometimes, when I have time, I leaf through my idea books and it fills me such inspiration that I want to start working on them all. And sometimes reading through them triggers even more ideas.

If you write down your ideas as soon as they are given to you (and I believe that ideas are a gift and they don't just spontaneously occur but are given) and add as much detail as you can, then you can let it go and get on with your current projects, safe in the knowledge that your idea is waiting for whenever you're ready.

Don't be afraid to writing too much when you're making notes for a new writing idea. Sometimes my notes go on for page after page and in the end it looks like I've already written a small novel. But, like I said before, you can never write too many notes.

And when you are ready to work on your next idea, and you have so many that you don't know which one to work on first, just chose the one that appeals to you the most and ignore the rest, for now.

This way, you can keep on storing ideas and keep writing too.

Sometimes, if I have an idea for an article or a short story, I'll just sit down and write it out in full. It doesn't matter how fast I write or if it's full of typos and grammatical errors, or I don't have a title. I just get write it as fast as I can while the complete thing is still in my head and use a working title.

I then know that my whole idea is saved and I can let it go and get on with my current writing.

Later, whether is a few hours later, or a few days, or even a few weeks later, I get out the piece of work, and go through it and tidy it up. I usually find that even more ideas pop into my head, but I try not to cram too many ideas into one short piece of writing. It's sometimes better to break it up into two short pieces writing, rather than one long tedious piece.

But as you write more, and you start keeping track of all your ideas, you'll find that it becomes such a habit that it's not difficult at all to have plenty of ideas for writing, whether you write online articles, short fiction, or complete book manuscripts.

Writing and finding ideas is like anything else we do in life. The more often we do it, the faster and easier it becomes. Athletes know exactly how to train to get the muscles they need. Musicians practice until they their fingers seem to work automatically. Likewise artists soon find their own style of work and can produce work effortlessly.

And it's the same for being a writer. The more you write, the easier and faster it becomes. I also believe that you need to read a lot too, and the more the read the faster you get with that too.

Just keep writing and the ideas will start to flow more easily and more often. I find that I get ideas from reading books. It only takes one sentence to spark an idea and I'll put down the book, pick up my ideas notebook and get my idea down in writing quickly so that I can carry on reading. I often read in bed and I even have a notebook and pen in my bedside drawer so that I can write down ideas fast, even if I'm reading at 2 am.

An idea is a gift. You don't expect it, you don't have to pay for it, it is simply given to you. Don't waste it. I find that no idea is ever wasted. Even ideas that I had years ago will eventually be used. Nothing is wasted.

Never waste an idea.

Even ideas can spark more ideas.

How To Do It All

By now you must be able to see how there is no need to have writer's block with so many places to find ideas and knowing how to store them when you have too many at once.

But how do you get it all written when you have so many ideas and so little time?

This can be a problem. You want to write but life keeps getting in the way. Even if you're a full-time writer it can still seem as though there are not enough hours in the day to write. And you wouldn't be wrong.

There's also the other problem that you want to write, but you can only manage to do it in short bursts.

Don't worry. All you have to do is take your time.

How many hours you write every day doesn't matter.

What does matter is how productive you are during those hours. Even if you feel you can only spare one hour a day to write, if it's a fully productive hour, it can still be enough. Writing only a page a day is one book written in a year.

Building a daily writing habit is more important than how much time you spend writing.

Every day we allot time to the things we have to do like going to work, picking the kids up from school, walking the dog, gardening, laundry, cleaning, cooking...the list goes on.

Yet writing is something that many people forget to make time for every day.

If you want to write, you have to make it a part of your daily program. Somewhere in your day there MUST be time for your writing.

If you don't feel that you have time in your hectic schedule for writing, then you'll have to get up earlier to write or go to bed later. Either way, you have to slot time for writing into your day, even if it means writing in your lunch hour at work or on the train or the bus.

Reading about other writers can be motivating and help keep you on track with your writing. Once you read about how they work and what they achieve, it can make you feel inspired to do the same.

Subscribe to other writers' blogs or websites and start reading about how they write. But don't try to do the same as they do. Aim to do more.

When you come across a writer who seems to write so much that they have seem to have more hours in a day than you do, don't get discouraged. The reason they write more than most others is because they've been doing it for a long time. The really prolific writers never stop writing. As soon as they finish one project they get straight onto the next without even thinking about the outcome from what they've already written.

They don't stop to think about how their book will sell, or who will read their online articles. They write because it's what they do, not because they expect a certain outcome and wait to see if it happens. They just jump from one project to the next and keep going, knowing that eventually, their previous work will find the right market.

And by that time they've written so many more articles and so many more books, that their passive income just keeps on growing while they just keep writing. And you need to do the same.

Stop worrying about whether your work is good, or how many people will read it, or whether people will criticize it or love it. You just need to keep writing. If you've written one book and it's selling through online bookstores, you'll earn money. If you have 10 books, you'll earn more. If you have 100 books you'll earn much more. So when you finish one book, publish it and start writing the next one, instead of sitting back and wondering how many sales you'll make from your previous book.

You job as a writer is to write.

Another thing to remember is to avoid distractions while you're writing or even before you begin, otherwise you won't even start. Make your writing time a priority and protect and preserve that time and don't let anyone or anything steal it from you.

Distractions are extremely harmful when you're writing in a window of creative genius, and you need to keep the flow going. If someone tries to talk to me, I say, "In the zone," without even looking up, and I keep on writing. If the phone rings, I look to see who it is, and if it's not someone important, I ignore it. But anyone who knows me knows not to call during office hours. I keep weekdays free to write, or to do anything else I want to do without interruption or apology.

If you have young children who need you, write when they're asleep. Kids go to bed early so it gives you plenty of time to write every evening. Prolific writers are organized writers.

Don't beat yourself up while you're writing. As long as you're writing, you're moving forward, so just start writing. If you think you're going wrong, keep writing. If you can't remember how to spell a word, spell it wrong. If you forget a name, write a reminder. Just keep writing. Never think you're doing badly. When you're writing, you're doing great.

Even if you sit and write furiously and end up having to delete most of the words, it's still writing and it's all part of the process. Just don't get angry with yourself. It happens to us all.

Sometimes, you can suffer from what is known as "creative monogamy" because you've been reading and working on the same idea for ages and all the mystery is gone and the jokes just don't seem funny anymore. And there's that critical voice in your head telling you that you're wasting your time and that your work isn't good, and you're so sick of working on the same project that you're inclined to agree.

But that doesn't mean that what you're writing isn't great. It's just that you've seen it so many times, especially when you've edited it and rewritten many parts several times. It gets to the stage where you're just sick of seeing it.

But stick with it. Remember that brilliant idea that triggered the whole thing off? Well, it's still there and your idea really is still that awesome. It's just that somewhere along the line you lost sight of your own awesomeness.

Just don't use it as an excuse to abandon what you're working on to start work on your next brilliant idea.

So What Happens Now?

Now you need to start finding ideas. Get yourself ready and start doing the necessary online research, go to your local library and start browsing all the books and magazines, start searching through online bookstores.

Your creativity is always there, it's just that sometimes, it needs re-igniting to make it spark. And once it does, get ready for a whole flood of ideas.

Just make sure that you're writing for yourself and not so that you can keep up with anybody else. While I might have said earlier that it's good to read about other writers and how they work, don't get too wrapped up in thinking that it's a competition.

"I do not try to dance better than anyone else. I only try to dance better than myself."
~ Mikhail Baryshnikov.

Go to bed every night feeling like you've made advancements with your writing, even it's just a couple of sentences. If you haven't done any writing you'll feel bad, that's why even writing just a few sentences makes you feel good because it feels like progress. And it is.

If you don't have time to start a new writing project, journal every day instead. Write down what you want to work on next, when you plan to start it, when you plan to finish and how you're going to go about working on it in between.

It's a great feeling at the end of the day to know that you've written something and are advancing in your writing and creating a daily habit.

Writer's block is usually nothing more than procrastination which is born from not knowing what to do next.

It's okay thinking that you want to write a book, but knowing where to start can be a problem and cause you to procrastinate.

But if you research and work the way I've already shown you, then procrastination won't be an issue.

You'll do your research, find some ideas, flesh them out and then write an outline from your notes.

Creating an outline for a book isn't difficult. Once you start organizing your notes and deciding on chapter titles and points to cover (or scenes to cover, in the case of fiction) in each chapter, and sub-points, it's then so easy to write your book.

And once you have you're outline, you're ready to start writing and that's when the fun begins. I always find that once I start a large writing project I'm eager to work on it every day.

But before I can get to that stage I need to know what I'll be writing, and this is why I always need an outline to work from. I can't be creative if I don't know where I'm going with what I'm writing. And most of my outlines are several pages long so they are really easy to follow and writing becomes effortless and fun.

And it all starts with that first spark of an idea. Sometimes I don't even know what I'm going to do with the idea or what it will end up being. It might be a series of articles for my website, an email series, a large eBook or a series of smaller eBooks.

But in the beginning it doesn't matter. I just need to write down my idea.

"You don't have to see the whole staircase, just take the first step."
~ Martin Luther King Jr.

Saying you have "writer's block" is just an excuse not to write. But as Stephen King (who I like to quote a lot) once famously said (and I paraphrase),

"Your muse won't show up for work until you do."

And it's true. All you have to do is make yourself sit down to write every day, even if you don't know what to write.

You could simply open up something you've been working on previously and re-read it or do a bit of formatting. Google the words "art gallery" and see if one of the paintings gives you an idea for a story. Take out a piece of writing that's written by someone whose work you really admire, and start writing it out by hand.

It doesn't matter what you do, as long as you write something.

So don't make any more excuses. If you previously didn't know how to spark your creative genius, you do now.

And if you need a little more inspiration, here are a few quotes about writing:

"I don't have to write. But if I didn't I wouldn't be very happy."
~ Mitch Levenberg

"I kept always two books in my pocket: one to read, one to write in."
~ Robert Louis Stevenson

"Your intuition knows what to write, so get out of the way."
~ Ray Bradbury

"Your imagination, my dear fellow, is worth more than you imagine."
~ Louis Aragon

"How to write: want to. Stop not writing."
~ Anne Lamott

"If I started to wait for moments of inspiration, I would never finish a book. Inspiration for me comes from a regular effort."
~ Mario Vargas Llosa

"Write what you want to write, worry about marketing them after they are done. You have no way of knowing what will be or is popular now or in one year or five years. When you listen to critical voice for anything, you are failing and not writing."
~ Dean Wesley Smith

"The ultimate inspiration is the deadline."
~ Nolan Bushnell

"The happiest of all lives is a busy solitude."
~ Voltaire

"If other people are putting in 40-hour work weeks and you're putting in 100-hour work weeks, then even if you're doing the same thing you know that you will achieve in 4 months what it takes them a year to achieve."
~ Elon Musk

"We are what we repeatedly do. Excellence then, is not an act, but a habit."
~ Aristotle

"The difference... between the person who says he 'wishes to be a writer' and the person who says he 'wishes to write'... the former desires to be pointed out at cocktail parties, the latter is prepared for the long solitary hours at a desk."
~ John Mortimer

"Lack of time is actually lack of priorities."
~ Tim Ferriss

"You don't get what you wish for, you get what you work for."
~ Brian Tracy

"The key to success is to start before you are ready."
~ Marie Forleo

"The way to get things done is to stop saying 'later' as in 'I'll do it later'. 'Later' is just another word for 'never'."
~ Ruth Barringham

End.

Thank you for reading.

To help you further, here is a list of recommended books. This are my own personal recommendations of books that helped me, and a couple of other books I've written that can help you.

Writing into the Dark: How to Write a Novel without an Outline
Dean Wesley Smith
https://amzn.to/3EKs1Vl

How to Write Pulp Fiction (Bell on Writing Book 10)
James Scott Bell
https://amzn.to/3Gq6cd0

How to have a 48 Hour Day
Don Aslett
https://amzn.to/2YbtGyw

Wake Up and Live!
Dorothea Brande
This book will help you reach your goals and achieve success
https://amzn.to/3gs6WU4

Think Like A Publisher: A Step-By Step Guide to Publishing Your Own Books
By Dean Wesley Smith
https://amzn.to/3Ex7KnD

How to Write an Article in 15 Minutes or less
- Including Research, Writing and Proof Reading
By Ruth Barringham
https://cheritonhousepublishing.com/books/15.html

7 Day eBook Writing and Publishing System
By Ruth Barringham
https://cheritonhousepublishing.com/books/7day.html

www.ingramcontent.com/pod-product-compliance
Lightning Source LLC
Chambersburg PA
CBHW050322010526
44107CB00055B/2352